SECOND THOUGHTS

Poems 2003 - 2013

Michael Baroff

2003

At Esalen

slowly undulating wave
floating
relaxing on the surface
breathing in and out
white foam bubbles up
pulse beat
fades away
to a blue layer of cloud
covering an otherwise clear sky

blow hole spurts
against the rocks
and rolls
tinsel covering
brightened white specks
lattice work webs
waves crossing

who were in those two chairs
facing each other
positioned for deep conversation

lady bugs me not
on the tree stump
crawling
pine cones dangle effortlessly
caring not if they fall
branches crisscross
holding each other tightly
shadows paint themselves
upon the lawn

you may think I'm not
thinking about you
but I am

2004

At Esalen

dreams burning
raging
with recent wounds
standing on the bridge
crying for more of what
I deserve

Back Home

maybe again next year
submit an idea
choose a date
wait for notice

constant hustle
anxiety
speaking out loud
to sympathetic ears

walk up and down
to the park
dogs
basketball

late night movie
again
love
death
drunken stupor
happy ending

on line
in a circle
across the square
so simple

calling out
for help
plea
please
ease the pain

giving up
giving in
becoming ordinary
enjoying what just is
choices catch up to you
after a while

whose thought
crossing my mind
wisdom
insight
television commercial
waiting
for what
for whom

who is this posterity
we are leaving it all for
positioning
against others
for a cause

I am so tired
of doing nothing

so, what's up
new moon
fog
singing vagabond
sitting in the corner

fiery red sky
on the wall
off the mark
inescapable
outward bound

whose job is it
anyway
not mine
obviously
you call that a debate
baseless
walk on
showcase
dress rehearsal

not knowing
the road
I ended up
where I am
lost again

sitting on the floor
no lotus
hunched over
time to be quiet
and scream
remembering

evil doing
loving
caring
hating
care free
fearful
ambivalent
ambiguous
sarcastic
kind
gentle
murderous
nurturing
so quiet
alone
and filled
with chaos

windmill
ceiling fan
air conditioning
I can breathe

we each have our rooms
doing what we do
alone
together

what else is there
the mind wanders
getting entertained
pushing away
the fear

take a walk
same streets
new day
old thoughts

serendipity
chance
change
no way
leave it
to what appears
accept or reject
unfolding
whatever the way
Tao to you
gone tomorrow

what's the big deal
about being prolific
just more stuff
to store

cross walk
down the line
to where
I revel
in what
I reveal

who do
you think
can ever
understand
this pleasurable
waste of time

a sampler course
bits and bites
only tastes
some digested
the remains excreted

here and there
is it somewhere
is it nowhere

one minute commercial
three minute song
thirty minute sitcom
one hour drama
two hour movie
all add up

surface engagement
tell and show
appearances take over
the underlying truth
that no one
will ever know

all the people
I have known
who are unknown

approach
avoid
near
far
have
hold
hello
hug
bye

alone at the beginning
rejected throughout
cling to connection
letting go
hurt and pain
loss
renewal
remembrance
forgetfulness after a while
thankfully

Sunday inside
looking outside
to which way
the wind blows
airplane engine buzz
harmonizes
with the stereo

rambling on and on
so insecure that something
might be left unsaid
let alone
understood

2005

set the stage
direct the action
facilitate the experience
include
respect
understand

everything in its box
organized
put away

flying high dream
floating above the room
dancing
twirling
arms outstretched
smiling

passion
discipline
practice
aesthetically pleasing
sometimes meaningful
just trying to make
a living

de-light-full
the light fill

on idle
idling
on hold
holding

progression
recession
repression
re-direction
permission
mutation
affection
ejection
erection
digestion
depression
expression
meditation
maturation

re-circle

another angle

square off

parallel process

Main and Ocean Park
Tues 4-19-05 2:06 pm

four pair of benches in a circle
only one sitter

ice cream eaters
saunter across the street
licking lips

where did the crow go
walked away
beyond the hedges

carrying backpacks and purses
searching around
to put in more

too warm for a hooded sweatshirt
she wears it anyway
admiring the bird of paradise

what's in her brown bag
left over lunch
a gift for a lover
prescription from the pharmacy

slim woman
cross back strap
long shirt
bare feet
sunglasses

infant held close
wrapped across mother's chest
sibling held by hand
all smiles

motorcycle rumbles
helmet on tight
bus kicks and screams

bicycle on the electric vehicle
just in case
the battery runs down

bird returns
flutters in the dirt
hole dug
flies away

two women with bags
one shopping
one homeless

bearded man
with cap on backwards
like a yarmulke

smile like a beauty queen
walks straight ahead

Getty Museum Sunday

sit
wait
look
listen

breeze
waterfall
chirping
conversations
others have

no rain
umbrellas for shade
stroll back and forth

LACMA Friday

museum jazz
Rauschenberg posters
collaged channel switch
Ethiopian protests for democracy
4.35% beer
vegetables abound

proposal sent
invites no response
four girls
three computers
chatting over
year book pictures

all these faces
could well have
been posted online
looking at each other
standing
staring
smiling
drinking
it all in

I'm hungry
no reason for take-out
I'll sit and eat here
with all these people
at a back table
facing out

expression still
holds my attention
who did what
now as it
has always been
sitting
silent
in thought
coming and going

warm breeze
children
hide and seek

2006

whiskey on the rocks
sushi on a plate
newspaper for a distraction
cup of water
geometrically placed rolls
piles of ginger and wasabi
first bite

two men with grey beards
first at the gallery
now at the restaurant
must be what we do
on a Saturday night alone

paid work
think and write
talk back
after listening
assumptions challenged
behavior changed

LA Times business section
Saturday April 8, 2006
 "robust job report drags down stocks'
explains it all

so many years divided
still it's the same
as it always was
and will be

cut up old art
mat and frame
new image
presented

no new messages
only old ones
heard before
saved and remembered

the other old man gone
left are the young girls
chattering about airline tickets

obsessed throwing out papers
magazines not worth their weight
mementos in boxes
saved too long

sitting here thinking about
what to do and not do
no big deal about winning
no score being kept

bought the 75 cent notebook
no wire coil to cut my finger
like the 50 cent one on sale

at night now quiet
thoughts to unfold
why is not a question

television amuses me
into a stupor
pleasure is all mine

flashing lights
smiles
crimes of passion

don't feel any remorse
seems to be destiny
after all these years
choices lead into a life

always something
new to do
if not
then what

it's gotten to be
that everyone
does everything
for their own purpose

of course it's a circle
no end
no beginning
just dizziness

please don't try to convince me
I care too much
to really care

your opinion
my opinion
layers of an onion
and then we cry

tarot on the sidewalk
predictions of future romance
after a refill

dream
he sat in the back seat
didn't want to commit suicide
just wanted to go along for the ride
at the intersection
we placed the tubes around his torso
unable to move
we rolled him down the incline
onto the street
where a car hit him
breaking his body up
we walked away
unnoticed

wisdom pulled
pain relieved
bite down freely

round table above the patio
waterfall contained in cement
coffee cup almost empty
floating mobile squares
shaded from the sun
people more back and forth

the phone rang this morning
no message left
as I soaked in the tub

repeated conversation
update on the here and now
open to future possibilities

it takes a day of hard work
to really be able to relax

more news of killings
sadness
pain
no solution

what I said was
this group creates intimacy
by picking a fight
so what if I don't feel it
we all are playing our roles
occasionally relating personally

pain in my neck
numbness in lower lip
vision blurry
thinning hair line
blood pressure high
it's great to feel alive

another one died today
almost died that is
shocked back to life
by the tears you shed

southern exposure needed
reception for all the channels
the wise man faces east

dead murderers remembered
war crimes revenged
no end to the insanity

hi
what's up
missed you

fixtures
laundry
passing by
sun sets

now that the work is done
what's left to do
but sit and wonder

giving good advice
to others
much easier
than taking it

what would I do
if I didn't sleep

I didn't see the crescent moon
crossing the bridge
you traveled

walk slowly
sit and look out

let go
fate in the hands of others
teeth filled
crowned
hip sways in pain
aches
new skin blemish

whose war is this now
we are all affected
scared and huddled
compassion
no longer only a choice

night time
right time
cloudy dark
book cover
opened
read
in the light

music on the grass
Congo beat
politicians in the air

summer only seems hot
inside its cool
and quiet

marketplace vegetables
bikes lined up
petitions to sign

coveted thought
unknown beliefs
laugh at the fool

what's relative is relevant
subjectivity is reality
knowing what you know
is the only known

really only a couple books
I would rely on if pressed
the rest
reminders of what
I once thought to be true

apartment dwellers
colleagues at meetings
people passing by
the few friends
daughter
lover
me

organized
by obsession
files
boxes
books
the TV
silent today

did I mention
it's conceptual art
showing up
asking questions
being consultative

she calls
asking the same question I had
is that our neighbor
on project runway

it's satisfying
to see
feel

imprint penetrates paper
Braille touch
on the other side

email greetings
a song programmed
content with the day
a hundred pounds of laundry
returns from summer camp
bare bones
sketched lines
water begins to boil

55
the speed limit
slow down
can it be possible
from the stationary position

on the elevator
he asked
coming from work?
no
I in worn jeans
say
from the market
you retired?
yeah
that's what I am
I reply

moments of confrontation
challenging inequity
questioning ambiguity
confidential
to whom
make it public
tell all

re-lax
re-educate
re-define
re-focus
re-assemble

death
rebirth
renewal
revision
line dot connects
meet me at the intersection
of now and then
float an idea
wrestle with it
pin against the mat
count to ten
I object to your object
declare victory

skip a page
left intentionally blank
go back and stare at it
until something appears

get up
shower
stretch
boot up

de-brief
be brief

that wild crazy
uninhibited man
crawling on all fours
howling at the moon
drooling
slobbering
in ecstasy
eyes a blaze
glaring

no concern about
staying within the lines
stretched surface
bold strokes
crazy lines
erased gestures
ripped pages

no need for drugs
madness will do
on its own
for now

pick up a book
read a few pages
believe its truth
for the moment

no self
worth its narcissism
could reflect
such beauty

boxed up the past
put away dreams
hidden desires
unknown pleasures

seeing patterns
accepting comfort
easing into joy
pleasure
happiness
contentment

mother gone eight years
leaving life behind
grateful for this moment

much less than
a half glass full
one gulp down

box of wishes
deposits made
arrangements secured
everything in place
for now

part time
work
girlfriend
parent

fewer pages left
to fill put
writing larger now

settling in again and again
words do not describe
what really is

prime time
now or then
waiting to fulfill destiny
time off for good behavior

much more
to clear out
empty
full
all in contrast

yesterday
a cosmic trigger
everything intensified
work search
love making
art for art's sake

observe lightly
express occasionally

pages ripped from below
tears flow down my cheek

stacked cards
fall on the floor
businesses scattered
all over the place

2007

Hollywood voice
indistinguishable
coast or continent
sounds to smooth
and persuade

please
fit in
to succeed
to survive

sleep to dream
work to live
watch it go by
dialogue
argue

align the line
what's my line
moving line
fine line
cross the line
broken line
straight line
squiggle line
dotted line
bold line
in line

time passes
we remain the same
looking at each other

crowds observe the walls
images hang for viewing
then and now defines it all
what reasons do we give
for how we are

balcony veranda
palm fronds grow
in a pot
bamboo covers the view

looking for work
asking to be invited
let me help
all I need is "thank you"

test taking for the future
entry into secret worlds
discover what is already known
who you meet
choices you make
out of my hands

sort through old drawings
arrange by theme
create some sort of continuity

enjoy hearing others talk
explore states of mind
process in action

what one does all day
repeat patterns
circles
habits

morning birds
awake earlier
than usual

what means to what end
the atmosphere is all around
moving in and out
returning to center

who to ask
who to see
how to be

comforts
without fear
of judgment

primary process
to smile
secondary process
to frown
stare out
breathe in

as long as
it makes
sense to me
is all
that matters
nothing to prove

shadow fog
silhouettes of palms
curtains cracked open

heart quiet
mind sad
alone in thought

images fake
memories
nothing
to hold on to

no philosophy
no word
sound it out
in gesture

combine what is
could be
never came true
allow fantasy
to sustain reality

whose process
mine
yours
ours
theirs

phone calls
short talks
thank you
for your interest

so many books
saying nothing new

enjoy amusements
for what
they are

quantum leap frog
jump over each back
repeat over again

a long walk
clears the head
tightens the muscles

mosquito
buzz
in my ear
swat away
continue
to write
bitten
blood
scratch
alcohol
skin
refreshed

clean off the patio
wait for the wash
to paint
the fresh look

fax letter
relay the mundane
hope all is okay
what else to say

create a presentation
who will see and hear
business outreach
work to do
for what

I really have
nothing much
to say
it's the coffee
that's kept me up

piece it together
adjust to being alone
flex left shoulder
prepare to get away
pay the bills
smile softly
walk forward

mystery without a solution
no formula to solve
until the story ends

next generation
ready
set
go

sure there are alternatives
options
don't let my cynicism
hold you back

no music just now
cars hum along the road
some voices
it's satisfying
to write
in the moment

images create
wonder
so abstract
it feels real

making soap
smell the fragrance
touch the skin
to heal
what about us?

in a dream
caught on the edge
falling over
seeking solace

waiting
wondering
wishing
no call
no text
not sleepy
espresso-ed

shadows
puppet show
moon light

electronic connections
to the outside world
in real time on tape
repetitive images
flicker away
lost memory

sunshine
my friend
warms
relaxes
remembers

waiting for
a call
a word
a look
a hug

closer to 60
than 50
what is
what wasn't
what could
have been

shadows on the wall
reflections on the water
ribbons of light

walk the streets
elemental particle
night air
digital display

thanksgiving
another day
family assembled
warmth for a time
two days from now

corrections
adjustments
resolution
for the new year
more whimsy needed

no point in re-reading
for sentence structure
to uncover meaning

fade in
fade out
natural course
in the dark
under the covers
awake

another phone message
"I do love you"
again unanswered

garage sale
knick knacks
possessed
stored
saved
some cherished

in the folder
ideas
a thought
a clever line
now and then
ready for the page

knowing
who I am
not knowing
what to do

batteries
run down
pressure up

no rain today
chill eve
slice of pie

accounting
adds up
more to
subtract

underwear on the carpet
dishes in the sink
alarm beeping
usual time
bathe
brushed
dressed
go be social

what can you really do
about your genetic make-up

start your engines
sing your song

trees hushed
voices snap
looking out to the street
another car passes by
door bangs shut
what is on the other side

calls not returned
from and to me

impulse
moves through
in
out
trust first impression
then stop

okay now
here it is
so what
there it goes

beat it
up
down
all around

chimes in the wind
sky writing
"I love you"

cross legged
pen in hand
squint at the page

airplane
help up
by string theory

palms trees trimmed
spring break
fire in Hollywood
waste paper
torn magazines
shredded
and trashed

isolated
not alone
connected
not dependent
that which is quick
is from all that
has been
culmination
not completion

I want to talk with you
in soft whispers
and gentle strokes;
spooned against your back
stroking your cheek
smiles and laughter
in the moment
forgetting everything else
that doesn't really matter
a deep breath
taking in the fragrance of skin
ours
only ours
hands clasped
fingers intertwined
knowing
all that we are together

frown unfurling
tentative gesture to the sun
breeze dances in sway
reflected shadow against chair

cross leg
clench jaw
dry skin knuckles
finger tips caress the page

"we talked about it"
overheard from the balcony above
honk, honk, honk, honk below

symptoms
dry cough
fatigue
sensitivity to sunlight

eyes closed
kaleidoscope vision
refracted blips and blurs

too much to share
all at once
best to keep it
close to home

vague images
dreams
thoughts
musings
personal myth
holds it all together
comfortable delusion

like my father
a solitary life
in own thoughts
putter about the day
walk in the neighborhood
listen to friends stories
child reserved
await escape
divorced from connections
depressed
yet smiling
waiting to die
and be released

2008

amidst the chatter
sparking lights
fire works
intricate patterns
unknown spaces
hovering beings
crescent bay
dark masses

in the field
grass
twigs
sunshine

such a relief
to submit
for now

possessions
remind me
who I made
myself
appear to be

what does it take
this time
to obliterate the past
start fresh
someplace else
some other people
why not

stripped away
rejected
starting up again
too tired to care
let's call it a day
heart pounds
still

is today the day
we sit across from each other
sipping coffee
talking about what is
laughing
forgetting what was
penniless
impoverished
without resources
destitute
no way out
prayer
what will it take
to continue this game

waiting
for what
hoping
for what
living
for what

potential opportunity
made the call
left a message

pushed away
ignored
unappreciated
like a pin ball game
ball bouncing
off the walls

rainy day
hot bath
quiet

2009

the end
done
did
finished
nothing left
spent

empty
nest
mind
cupboard
pockets
look into my eyes
is there anyone there today
if so
come out and play

who says
it has
to be
chronological

a handful care
laugh and smile
prophecy comes true
death be welcome
no big deal
done before
will occur again
no call back
last try
cash in
give up
give in
close out
close the book
did my best
not enough
passed by
passed on
no way out
out of steam
most will forget
gone fishing
lights out
no one home

found these blank pages
makes as much sense
as anything else
oh yeah
it's my birthday
again
still working it out

bought haiku book
reading other's words
writing my own now

years pass by
names and places
mostly forgotten

asleep
while awake
missing your
smile
voice
touch

helping another
to help myself
feel it will be okay

light and darker now
no fog today
maybe tomorrow

pictures flash by
crickets provide
the sound track

boxes
books
paper
data discs
computer recycled
hope my identify is safe

eight years ago
two more to go
fulfill a prophecy

do you recall my face
I see your body
all too distant

staying inside
too much stimulation
out there

suddenly no more thoughts
about the future
only now

dried flowers
a valentine from you
so long ago

small objects
adorn shelves
to remind me

flick of the wrist
pen stoke
drawn line

camera lens
opens
zoom in
out
automatic focus

short walk
so satisfying

confidential illusion
while it lasts

nice to talk
on the phone
once in a while

sorting through stuff
boxes moved
back and forth
now I know
where everything is

happy holidays
call next year
two months from now

everything
and everyone
I have turned away
turned off
what is left

my own thoughts
occupy too much
space and time

4:54 am
darkness outside
sadness inside

cannibalize thoughts
eating inside out
a smile
a touch
keeps me awake
wanting

intermittent thoughts
inconsequential

at least
I have some work
on the books
coming month
fuller than usual
can that become usual
oh man
I want
to be
touched
today

who will call
or not
who knows
who cares

left to my own devices
another day
year

what's changed
what's the same

squawk
hum
fog
clack
snap
clap
squeak
chirp
street sounds
coming to a stop
now
moving along
warm cheek
eyes
lips close
pressure in ears
thumb bent writing

almost over
year end
nothing to lose
or win

incense smell
left over
in proximity

2010

begin relaxed
focused
attentive
alive
happy

balcony chair
sea air
sunshine

2011

no sweat
tired early eve
last night in Ojai
sweat my prayers in lodge
youth around
calling out admonitions
hurt and pain
sadness and loss
hunger for creativity and passion
we are all human

Elder
who me
wish I knew
anything

distractions
get
keep
me down

still trying to give it away
uhm
donations
received
another reminder
of the "now"

it comes down
to just accepting
what is
and
keeping open
to what might be
a mystery

scheduling work
time for a hair cut

who says it's "process"
it's all inner work
right

the tight moment
right person
right thought

it's a real pain
being so damn
philosophical
I think I'll just
meditate
 "change yourself
change the world"
it's said

ho hum
what's on
the agenda
the list
to do

ennui
a motivation
to change

who shall I be
today
tomorrow
the next day
resolved
I am me
no way out

it is necessary
for anyone
to know
what I did
enough that I know
it's my scorecard
after all

nice to be acknowledged
does require action
overt notice
intermittent reinforcement
enough to keep going
not enough to feel good
at least I can smile
at myself

can it really be a mystery
better than tragedy
always comedy

another sunset
takes so little
to feel alive again

conversations
getting out
doing good work

along the way
I forgot
again

love lost
heart broke
still so sad

where is the motivation
needing a nudge

certainly stuck
repetitious movement
unanswered questions
lost visions
commonplace
who can I help now
without leaving home

sacred undertaking
no fear of death
only pain

no walk today outside
on the tread mill

simple routines
repeated over
and over and over
again every day
washed clothes
whether needed
or not
satisfying task
always

brush my gray hair
looking in the mirror
from all angles

sit cross-legged
straight back
eyes closed
in the dark
giving up
let everyone else
succeed

more to strip away
getting it in order
leave little behind
only what really matters

how do I make it
through each day
thank god for philosophy
a good concept provides
needed rationalization
abstraction is timeless
nothing needs to change

if depression is the norm
only up to go
baseline measurement
flat line
tow the line
out of line
get in line
stay in line
next in line

getting to the point
of no return(s)

warrantee expired
own the merchandise
un-planned obsolescence
do what you can with it

more gestures
figments of vision

making the best
of a no-way out
situation
with moments left

too many opinions
that don't really matter
flip the switch

past midnight
heart beat
remembering
not so simple
let life show up
however
whenever
who ever
cry out loud
to be heard

collect thoughts
tie with twine
preserve
for future generations
as if they will care

no novel
no journal
just words

around and about
round about
get around
get by
get high
no lie
I spy (with my eye)
do try
give in
up
so smart
outsider
outlier
poser
fake
fraud
sleep it off
enough already
of not enough

picture this
if you will
being who
doing what

direction
trajectory
target
hit or miss
no matter

pared down
into pairs

quiet mind
stripped bare
open
vulnerable
what's there to hide

being helpful
once in a while

waiting to be early
prepared
for the unanticipated
now
big smile

what's the point
be sharp
condense
edit
get to the point
more precisely

fantasies sustain
the reality
of failure

in my mind
I succeed
older
wiser
if only

not knowing
is enough
to get through
another day

countdown
countless
yesterdays
some tomorrows

it's only a number
who's counting
congratulations

oblivious
clouds
dark horizons
holes dug
tripped in
over and out

simultaneous underpinnings
forgotten motives

concrete endeavors
sanctimonious illusions
covet operations

glory be the sounds
pushed and peddled
no organ transplant tonight

cheer to all
revelations
tight space
ingenuity prevails
carried away
unnoticed
no worries

let's begin now
Joshua Tree
heat
quiet
gentle breeze

twilight time
transition hour
sip a beer

are you retired she asked
sometimes I think I am

another day
floating in warm pool
moon and sun above
heart beats strong

not so much going on
waiting
for something to change

so many gestures
was it a question you asked
was it a statement
to be left unanswered
all I know is that
I want to connect
with you
so I responded

2012

hiatus
procrastination
anticipation
resolved

what is it I want
maintenance free
allowing
surrendering to what is
give in and up
taking what comes
come what may
May December

give me something
to push against
so to be responsive

a year passes
milestones
mill stones
anchors
delusion of humility
wanting for what
else may come along

same conversations
with myself
putting off
taken for granted
by myself
not so deep

no fault
no harm
no worry
no thing

gibberish
nonsense
glittering generalities
all rise to the surface
of my thoughts

eliminate
cull
shed
trash
minimize
simplify
edit

longing
long and short of it
short changed
left out
down and out
over and out

without you here
I'm not so sure

2013

reprieve
regroup
re-energize
re-focus

borderline
empty days
repetitive actions

can't seem to get out of it
one constructive action a day
list the opportunities
over and over again
make a call
send emails
hesitate to follow-up
submit a proposal
wait wait   wait

is it process
or procrastination

self portrait
ablaze in calm tension
illusion of something or other
delusion that something
will change

all the same
looking out for myself
looking out at myself

to know
to die
to decay

diverted
distracted
deluded
dismissed
disregarded
desired

the phone does not ring

accidental
unintended
serves the purpose

give up
give in
give it
away

first day of summer
stuck
reach out
empty
only ideas
left alone
to my own devices
healthy yet lost
hopeless
moments of energy
wake up in the middle to the night

fall apart
tape together

I did try
I really did
best I can

can I survive with
what I have
what I think
what I feel
what I do

walking out the door
each puddle invites
a closer look

tiny leaf
hangs down
near the knot

cars rushing by
her eyes stare back
without acknowledgment

the building sign weathered
protected from the rain
a tide pool of cracked wood

today's mail gone
a blast of sun
warm my cheek

melodious bells ring
for a moment
the noise of the street
silent

how safe is the cracked payment
my feet step high
avoiding the danger
dare I cross the street
pushing the button
I wait
then process

locked gate
keeps me out
not a member here
dark oak tree stands tall
guarding
to protect what
through the fence
golfers traipse across the greens
setting up
to be teed off
 "take a swing" it reads

chill wind
drizzle
when will the light
change

purple flower
what's your name
no matter
you are beautiful and fragrant

trash cans
water hose
staked chairs

taking a whiff
mango passion fruit
before submerging
into the hot water
wait before I drink

what can be said
from without
what can be shared
from within

sounds in the air
fuzzy head this morning
almost time to dance
be bop
hip hop
flip flop

atop a rock
sitting
cool air
bugs and birds

jump in
step back
proceed

candid conversations
need another person